LOGICAL UNDERSTANDING OF THE SUPREME

(BASED ON BHAGAVAD GITA CHAPTER-7)

DR. JAGADEESH PILLAI

Contents

Prayer

HARE RAMA HARE RAMA, RAMA RAMA HARE HARE - HARE KRISHNA, HARE KRISHNA, KRISHNA KRISHNA, HARE HARE

(Mantra - Kali Santaranopanishad)

Dedicated To

|| All THOSE WHO ARE KEEN TO UNDERSTAND THE SUPREME ||

Preface

This book help to deeply understand the power and presence of the Supreme and its divinity. To achieve the same continues connection with the Supreme, strong desires and feeling its presence everywhere is required.

There is nothing more to learn and achieve once you understood the reality of the Supreme by the wisdom of your experience.

Only one person from a thousand is trying to understand the Supreme and from such thousand and thousands of persons only one hardly understands the reality of the Supreme.

About The Author

Dr. Jagadeesh Pillai a voracious reader, Four Times Guinness World Record holder, writer, and true research scholar was born in Varanasi, the abode of Lord Shiva. He is Ph.D. in Vedic Science. He is a multi-faceted polymath with innate qualities, creative ideas and many remarkable achievements. Although his roots extend back to "Gods own Country"(Kerala), the residents of Varanasi feel proud of him and adore him as a child of Varanasi who caters to every individual in need without any expectations. A deep study into his profile reflects that he has added so many feathers to his cap which makes him quite unique. He is a four times Guinness Book of World Records Holder in the following subjects :

"Script to Screen" which he achieved by producing and directing a state of art animation film within the shortest time possible by breaking the earlier set record by Canadians. There are many national and international Awards and Recognitions to his credit.

Longest Line of Post Cards which he has done on the occasion of 163 years of Indian Postal Day by 16300 post cards. The event was also connected with a questionnaire about Indian Flag.

Largest Poster Awareness Campaign – This was achieved by designing an awareness campaign on the subject "Beti Bachao – Beti Padhao".

Largest Envelop – Towards tribute to Prime Minister's initiative 'Make in India' – he has created about 4000 sq meter envelop using waste papers.

Attempted by lighting 70000 candles on a 210 kg cake to celebrate the 70th Indian Independence day recorded in World Records India.

Attempted a documentary on Dhamek Stupa of Sarnath dubbing in 17 languages, result is waiting from Guinness World Records.

He is versatile in Gita teaching. The young generation is fond of his Gita teaching and he has changed the life of many young through his continued motivational boost up and teachings.

He has composed and sung Gayatri Mantra in 1000 different tunes.

He has composed and sung Hanuman Chalisa in 108 different tunes.

He has composed and sung hundreds of Sanskrit Bhajans, Patriotic songs, etc.

He has written and directed so many short films and documentaries for awareness campaigns.

He has done voluntary services to UP Police and Kerala Police to spread awareness campaigns on the various issue through videos and photography.

He is on the path of authoring thousands of books on Indian culture, Indian Temples, and the life of extraordinary people.

It is hard to believe that he has produced and directed more than 100 Documentaries on a particular city (Varanasi) which is done by a single person.

He has helped and guided more than 25 boys and girls to achieve world records through various creative and innovative methods.

A multifaceted person who can apply the best of his intellect using the God-given blessings which have been showered upon every human being granting them an immense capacity to learn, experience, and experiment with many things and do wonders in this world of discrimination and disparities.

He is a teacher and a student at the same time who always learns every day and teaches every day. As a master, his weakness was that he never sticks to a particular subject. Perhaps this weakness gives him the strength to master any area which he came across.

Each of his days dawned with learning a new topic and he spend most of his time experimenting and researching it.

He is also a selfless social activist and a motivational speaker.

His life was full of struggle, ups and downs, and failures. But he never gave up and faced all his trials and tribulations full of confidence. Today he is a successful young man with a lot of enthusiasm and rich life experience.

He has sung full Ram Charita Manas 51 hours audio by his own composition. He has also sung the whole Bhagavad-Gita in his own composition with a rhythmic background.

He has also sung "Lokah Samastha Sukhino Bhavantu" in 50 different languages.

Currently working on a detailed and scientific study on Veda, Upanishad, Puranas, Bhagavad Gita, etc.

Currently, he is the Hon' Chancellor of 'Eurasia Digital University'.

Awards

Four Times Guinness World Records

Winner of Mahatma Gandhi Vishwa Shanti Puraskar

Mahatma Gandhi Global Peace Ambassador
Kashi Ratna Award

Dr. APJ Abdul Kalam Motivational Person of the Year 2017

Mother Teresa Award

Indira Gandhi Priyadarshini Award

Bharat Vikas Ratna Award

Udyog Ratna Award

Vigyan Prasar Award

Poorvanchal Ratn Samman

LOGICAL UNDERSTANDING OF THE SUPREME

Chapter-7 and Chapter-8 of Bhagavad Gita is connected with Chandogyopanishad. A deep study of this Upanishad will help to understand these chapters very easily.

This chapter is based on one of the Mahavakyas "The Great Sayings" "TATWAMASI" of Samved.

Tat – That

Twam – You

Asi - are

We have already gone through various examples and understood that the ultimate authority of everything in the universe is the Supreme.

Now onwards we are going to deeply understand the power and presence of the Supreme and its divinity. To achieve the same continues connection with the Supreme, strong desires and feeling its presence everywhere is required.

There is nothing more to learn and achieve once you understood the reality of the Supreme by the wisdom of your experience.

Only one person from a thousand is trying to understand the Supreme and from such thousand and thousands of persons only one hardly understands the reality of the Supreme.

We have already discussed about the different group of people from lower level to upper level in one of the previous chapters. So only those curious group people who after enjoying all the lavishness in many life when they won't find mental satisfaction and permanent peace, they will search for the reason of it and that search finally arrives them to under the reality of the Supreme.

***

There are two kinds of nature.

NATURE-1 - ***Visible***

The nature is created with Earth, Water, Fire, Air, Space, Mind, Intelligence & Ego.

All the species, many other physical and material things and whatever happenings on the earth is because of that.

NATURE -2 - ***Invisible***

The Supreme.

All activities in Nature-1 is happening because of the The Divinity of the Supreme which is embedded in every creation of it.

A small atom of Nature-1 can disturb the whole world because each and every atom contents the divinity and power of the Supreme, *(recall the days of lockdown during Covid-19).*

***

The whole world is the result of Nature-1 & Nature-2

Nature-1 is the Creations/Generations

Nature-2 is the Generator/Creator, Operator and Destroyer

Eg : Nature-1 is our Body, but without Nature-2, it will be deadbody.

Means..

Nature-1 + Nature-2 = an active body with Soul.

When Nature-2 (divinity-soul) withdraws from Nature-1, the existence of Nature-1 (body) ends.

Every creations of Nature-1 (physical and material things) is connected with Nature-2 (the Supreme) like pearls in a garland.

Eg :

NATURE-1 (Creations)

NATURE-2 (The Supreme)

Water

Power of quenching the *thirst*

Sun/Moon

Power of lightening

Every Knowledge & Wisdom

Omkar (the divine words/secrets)

Space

Sounds & Thunder

Human

Humanity within (virtues)

Earth

Smell of it, smell every flowers, taste of every fruit, etc.

Fire

Flames & quality of purification

Every species

Divinity/Soul within

Striving and dedicated selfless hardworking people to achieve something beneficial to others

Power, Energy and concentration within them

Origin of every Species

Permanent Seed and cause of creation

Great Scholars

Intelligence

People who have expanded their talents, by extensive intelligence and wisdom and respected by a large audience around the world.

Their Grace

People with Ethical thoughts and action

Power & Strength to do ethical things

People who does selfless actions towards obligatory duty

Fulling Ethical Desires

Apart from the above, the three Gunas (Satvik, Rajasik & Tamasik) are also originated from the Supreme and but that possess by its creations (Nature-1) but the creator Supreme (Nature-2) hasn't posses any of it.

The Supreme is permanent and its actions are also permanent and invisible. It's divinity, blessings and energy are equally distributed to everybody. Since he has no change in his actions, no guna he possesses.

The human and few other creations on the earth changes its actions, attitude and habits to fulfil their selfish desires, attachment, ego, etc. because of the these three Gunas.

When a person frees from all kinds of Tamasik & Rajasik guna actions, only Satvik Guna (ethical/divine qualities) in every action of him remains. Then when he constantly by concentration and meditation trying his best to stick into Satvik Guna in each and every action, he will be liberated to higher level and will be qualified as "Karma Yogi – Qualified Soul" or "Karma Sanyasi" level.

Satvik Guna contents divine quality which inspire us to do more and more selfless action (Nishkam Karma) and if a person continuesly possess this quality in each and every action of him, his divine quality will be increased. Divine quality increasing means, a lot of talents, ideas, intelligence, wisdom which was hidden earlier because of Tamasik and Rajasik guna will boost up.

Qualities of Satvik Guna (Group of people with Divine Qualities)

1. Facing every adverse situation with peace of mind.

2. Mental Purification.

3. Wisdom and understanding of Body, Soul with mind and senses

& the Supreme.

4. Reading and research a lot to understand the power of the

Supreme.

5. Concentrate and wisely think before doing any action.

6. Be in a meditate mode to take quick wise decisions.

7. Non-violence by mind, word & actions.

8. Speaking about reality and truth of life.

9. Controlling mind and senses while doing every action.

10. Desireless in unwanted objects.

11. Gentleness, silence, patience and down-to-earth behaviour.

12. Absence of pride on his talents.

13. No leg pulling rather promoting, motivating each and

everybody.

14. Trying to expand his level of action by developing, innovating,

creating, discovering, inventing various things which are

beneficial to the world.

15. Will be a great scholar and people will be attracted to avail the

light of wisdom from him.

16. Controlled attachment with family, relationship, wealth, etc.

17. High Virtues, quality of balancing, holistic, positive and

peaceful.

Opposite to above will come under Rajasik & Tamasik Gunas.

Chapter-14 explains in detail about all three Gunas

***

It is very difficult for a common man to follow Satvik guna by crossing the illusion of worldly pleasures, desires, bondage and attachments with physical and material desires etc.

By continues practise in applying Satvik guna in each and every actions, and when on get mastry on it, he will cross the level of Satvik also and will achieve either Karma Yogi *(Qualified Soul)* or Karma Sanyasi *(Qualified to renunciate Karma)* status, the quality and status as the Supreme.

Rajasik and Tamasik Guna followers (the ignorant minds), wont be able to understand the wisdom and intelligence of the Supreme, hence they don't get the status of a Karma Yogi or Karma Sanyasi and not the status same as the Supreme.

***

There are four kinds of people who worship God for their wish fulfilling.

1. Patiens with Physical & Psychological Problems

Diesese, mental problems, stress, disappointments, suffering

from break ups, loneliness, sorrows, etc.

2. People who are curious to get wisdom and understanding.

Wisdom seekers, enquiring and in search of answers to few

questions like who am I, Why I am here, What exactly I have

to do, etc.

3. Money minded people

Always with a keen desire to make more wealth and money.

Even if they earns, wont be spending even for their

requirements. They will be satisfied collecting, earning and

saving lot of money.

4. Wisdom achieved scholars (Karma Yogi status).

They are already understood the power of the Supreme and

does every action for the Supreme or being done the actions

like the Supreme.

***

Out of the all above, first three are the souls on their developing stage and they choose various other ways of worship comfortable for them just to fulfil their selfish desires and wishes.

But on the other hand the 4th level wisdom achieved scholars wants to achieve the Supreme only and so they does actions for the Supreme, as the Supreme for the benefit of all.

Its like a doctor likes, respect and understand a doctor, an advocate likes, respect and understand an advocate, a millionaire likes, respect and understand millionaire, a poor person likes, respect and understand a poor, a student likes, respect and understand a student, a teacher likes, respect and understand a teacher, a scholar likes, respect and understand a scholar

And

the Supreme likes, respect and understand a qualified scholar (Karma Yogi or Karma Sanyasi) who does every action like the Supreme.

From the above, once again we are getting a strong message from God/the Supreme that who does Supreme Quality actions for the benefit of all, the Supreme likes them.

One has to take several births to achive the level as the Supreme so such kind of scholars are very rarely available in our surroundings. May be one in a millions or so.

See, we all are eager to make immense wealth, properties, billions and trillions of money, etc. and to achieve all these are not easy, we need to hardwork, maintain health and sacrifice a lot.

But nobody is eager to achieve the most valuable/ultimate thing in the universe which one cannot buy with anything, i.e. the Supreme.

Yes, we need to only sacrifice some un-necessary attitude and habits and try to achieve the wisdom and intelligence to understand the Supreme. Once we achieve this, nothing else has left to be achieved because we will have the power of the Supreme and will be able to do Supreme actions which will remain permanent and will be beneficial for all.

***

Regarding the concept of God worshipping of following people:

1. Patiens with Physical & Psychological Problems.

2. People who are curious to get wisdom and understanding.

3. Money minded people.

To fulfil their selfish desires, comforts, enjoyments, worldly pleasures, and to accumulate wealth and properties, they will mis-use (wasting) their intelligence per their guna nature and they worship different God's per their imagination and concept.

and

the Supreme helps to fix their faith in their concept of God worshipping and they reap the results also. But the worshippers has a false belief that the blessing are given by the God of their concept, but the fact is that the blessings and result has come from the Supreme itself because everythying on the earth, even the different God concepts are also connected with the Supreme.

The results and blessings they gets by the Supreme through the God of their concept depends per their intention, devotion, mental purification etc. (partially fulfills).

The partial result/benefits which are achieved by the ignorant worshippers through their different God concepts are not going to be permanent. It has a low life and will expire any time. That's why there are so many people who worship God of their concept everyday for hours through different methods and offerings but they are unable to make any remarkable changes in life.

Since, their concept of God, their desires all are of selfish nature to fulfil many of their physical and material gains, they has a false belief that God (the Supreme) also exists in a physical form. But the fact is that the Supreme is formless.

The ignorant people afflicted with false illusions of worldly pleasures are unware about the invisible form of the Supreme which is permanent and imperishable and nobody would be able to visualise it through the eyes. We cannot see an atom through our open eyes and the Supreme may be a trillions and trillion of times smaller than that.

UPANISHAD SAYS THE SIZE OF BRAHMAN

The wisdom achieved scholars, whose intentions are purely selfless and beneficial to all, won't follow a different God concept and worshipping. They will directly connect with the Supreme to get the blessings to expand their field and level of action.

They achieve the Supreme itself.

***

Being the Generator, Operator and Destroyer of every creature in the universe, the Supreme knew in advance about all the future effects and results which are going to happen. It also mean that the Supreme pre-decides the result of our action whatever we does, per our intention behind it.

Suppose, we attended an examination in the school and we have to go to the school for the result next month. But the teacher already verified the answersheet and given the marks. The teacher already knew it many weeks ago before we gets the progress report. In the progess report there is a red mark given for some indisciplinary activity done in the school. We were unaware about it, so we asked the teacher. The teacher has shown us a CCTV footage of three months ago which proves that we did an indisciplinary activity in the school.

So the teacher in advance knew the marks and knew about the indisciplinary actitivy which was reflected in the progress report and whenever you see it or show it to anybody in the future, the red mark for the indisciplinary activity done by you will remain there.

The teacher is not responsible for whatever less mark you got in the exam and for the red mark. We, our performance and actions are responsible for the result we got.

Same way, the Supreme is not responsible for any result we gets in life. Our performance, actions and intention behind it are responsible for the result.

So whatever we are doing today, the result may come in our life in different ways and in different time. The result may not come as we expected rather it will reflect later in our life per our intention behind it. We cannot calculate it in advance.

Suppose we catched a butterfly which was flying in the garden and we killed it curely by putting it on a fire of flame. The butterfly was innocent and was an excellent creation of the Supreme. It was created to fulfil some duites which it has assigned by the Supreme. But when we killed it cruely and intentonally, we destroyed two things, a creation (Butterfly) and its action (Butterfly's Karma).

For us, a Butterfly was a little thing and we forgot the incident also.

At the same moment when we were killing the Butterfly, we have already generated our punishment too which will reflect in our life later sometime as unexpected incidents.

Quote to note :

So whenever there is an effect of an unexpected adverse situation in our life, there must be a cause behind it.

A Life example :

There was a large wholesaler of marbles. He was supplying it to various distributors around the state. Once or twice in a month, the distributors will come and meet the wholesaler to pay the balance amounts of bills. One distributor was not regular in payments and because of that the wholesaler used to abuse the distributor very badly. Whenever the distributor comes to meet the wholesaler, his son of eighteen years old was also accompanied him. The wholesaler used to scold and abuse the distributor in front of his son.

After few years that distributor has expired because of some health issues and his son taken the charge of him.

After few years, one day evening, the son of the distributor (now he is in the age of 23) has visited the wholesaler to make some payments which his father owes him. But immediately that boy attacked the wholesaler with a hammer and run away. The wholesaler was killed on the spot.

The wholesaler was a God believer, he and his family used to go to the temples and also done charities.

The intention behind going to the temples and doing the charity was to flourish his business and to protect his family. It was not for the benefit of the whole world.

Being a wholesaler, the egoistic feeling of being bigger than a normal distributor, his attitude towards the distributors was very unpleasant.

Why the wholesaler was killed by the boy? Because the wholesaler was abusing his father in front of him. The boy was always visualised and experienced it and felt very bad that his father was humiliated and injured their dignity and pride. At the same moment, the anger and feeling of revenge was initiated in his mind of that boy which resulted to kill the wholesaler by the boy after few years.

Now the family of the wholesaler has lost the faith in God and stopped worshipping God going temples, etc. because they believe that God has no power and their worshipping to God and their charities are not helped.

So, its clear that their faith on God and God worshipping was for their own safety and wish fulfilments. If the results or situations are against their expection, then no God exists.

They won't ready to accept that the attitude towards a distributor was the reason.

Now

Is it acceptable or commandable that the boy has done? No.

He should not do that.

This is what we discussed in previous chapters to balance the mind, practise forgiveness, etc.

The battle of life and actions are like that.

Wholesaler abused because the distributor was not regular in giving payments and makes so many excuses always. So there is a reason, why the wholesaler irritated or abused. The wholesaler never stopped business with the distributor, he used to help always even his payments was irregular.

So, the boy has to understand that we are wrong in our part that's why we are liable to accept abuses from the wholesaler.

Facing such situations of abuses, mental conflics, anger, feeling of revenge etc. are the actions we should control and overcome without reacting it with a wrong action from our side.

Result : *Wholesaler lost his life & the boy is in Jail.*

Who won and who lost. "Nobody"

Options to avoid conflicts :

1. The wholesaler had an option to stop business with him through mutual discussion for mutual benefit if the distributor is irregular in payments for a long time. But if still decided to continue business with him, then forgive it and manage silently when he is irregular in payments. Continuing business with him and abusing him when he is irregular is not a good option.

2. The boy has to advise his father to do regular payments to the wholesaler to avoid abuses from him or to stop business with him.

3. The boy has to understand that the wholesaler is always distributing and helping his father even if he makes irregular payment, so considering the help of wholesaler, the boy has to fogive him.

Managing through Wisdom and Intelligence

1. Do business for the benefit of all with peace and harmony. Avoid adverse situations intellectually without any harm to anybody. Abuses will impure the mind. We are are temporary care taker here and have to leave all the physical and material things, even the family just after few years. Every distributor must be very happy because satisfied distributors are the backbone of a wholesaler.

The boy has to think that he is nobody to punish anybody in the world. The owner and authority of all the creature on the earth is the Supreme. Human actions are based on the guna dominace so the human has no authority to estimate or even think whether a person doing good or not. A human automatically generates the blessings and punishment based on his intention behind every activity.

Better to connect directly to the Supreme and submit all our mind disturbances to him without reacting to it.

***

When we born and brought up with a body, the fight starts when we are happy by fulfilling a desire and feel sorrow when we are unable to fulfil the desire. Achieving a desire has given ultimate happiness and when it was unable to achieve, extreme sorrow and anger develops. While in anger, our intelligent doesn't work properly and take evil decisions/actions. The fruit of evil actions will generate more and more bad faces in life.

The whole life cycle from birth to death goes like "feeling good when something achieves and feeling sad when we are unable to achieve", in between throughout the life, never ever we think about the Supreme, the creator of us and everything. Never ever even think why we are actually born, what is the purpose of our life. This is called ignorance and foolishness. We lived the whole life without understanding and the reality of the ultimate authority, its existence, form, authority and forgets the real obligatory duties which has to be performed.

There is a great verses there written by Shankaracharya in his ultimate poem of wisdom "The Bhaja Govindam"...

Balastavat Kreedaasakthaha

Tarunastavat Taruneesakthaha

Vridhastavat Chintaasakthaha

Pare brahmani ko pi na saktaha

The childhood we lost in games, The Youth, we lost with the thought of girls, The old age we passes with worry and anxiety thinking over many things. But nobody at nowhere thought about the existence of the self and the Supreme.

***

All those wisdom achieved scholars who understood the reality of the Supreme and connects with it, does all their selfless actions with a purified mind towards dedication to the Supreme. Instead of worshipping many Gods, all of their actions (karmas) itself are like worshipping the Supreme, so there are no sins generates to them.

As mentioned earlier, all actions first originates in the mind & senses, mind & senses are connected with the Soul and the Soul is connected with the Supreme.

So, whatever we even image, think, speak or act....will touch the Soul and the Supreme. When we image, think, speak or act negatively, we generates bad karma (sins and curses). But if we image, think, speak or act good, we generates (boons and blessings).

So the wise scholars does all of their karmas towards dedication to the Supreme with a purified mind and enjoys life with ultimate satisfaction and permanent peace without any kind of regret even when in a death bed.

***

[illegible] childhood we [illegible] of thoughts or [illegible] we passed [illegible] and [illegible] thinking [illegible] many things. [illegible] never thought about the existence of [illegible] Supreme.

[illegible]

[illegible]

[illegible]

So the wise scholars [illegible] Supreme [illegible] with ultimate [illegible] without any kind of [illegible] even when [illegible]

1

śhrī bhagavān uvācha
mayyāsakta-manāḥ pārtha yogaṁ yuñjan mad-āśhrayaḥ
asanśhayaṁ samagraṁ māṁ yathā jñāsyasi tach chhṛiṇu

2

jñānaṁ te 'haṁ sa-vijñānam idaṁ vakṣhyāmyaśheṣhataḥ
yaj jñātvā neha bhūyo 'nyaj jñātavyam-avaśhiṣhyate

3

manuṣhyāṇāṁ sahasreṣhu kaśhchid yatati siddhaye
yatatām api siddhānāṁ kaśhchin māṁ vetti tattvataḥ

4

bhūmir-āpo 'nalo vāyuḥ khaṁ mano buddhir eva cha
ahankāra itīyaṁ me bhinnā prakṛitir aṣhṭadhā

5

apareyam itas tvanyāṁ prakṛitiṁ viddhi me parām
jīva-bhūtāṁ mahā-bāho yayedaṁ dhāryate jagat

6

etad-yonīni bhūtāni sarvāṇītyupadhāraya
ahaṁ kṛitsnasya jagataḥ prabhavaḥ pralayas tathā

7

mattaḥ parataraṁ nānyat kiñchid asti dhanañjaya
mayi sarvam idaṁ protaṁ sūtre maṇi-gaṇā iva

8

raso 'ham apsu kaunteya prabhāsmi śhaśhi-sūryayoḥ
praṇavaḥ sarva-vedeṣhu śhabdaḥ khe pauruṣhaṁ nṛiṣhu

9

puṇyo gandhaḥ pṛithivyāṁ cha tejaśh chāsmi vibhāvasau
jīvanaṁ sarva-bhūteṣhu tapaśh chāsmi tapasviṣhu

10

bījaṁ māṁ sarva-bhūtānāṁ viddhi pārtha sanātanam
buddhir buddhimatām asmi tejas tejasvinām aham

11

balaṁ balavatāṁ chāhaṁ kāma-rāga-vivarjitam
dharmāviruddho bhūteṣhu kāmo 'smi bharatarṣhabha

12

ye chaiva sāttvikā bhāvā rājasās tāmasāśh cha ye
matta eveti tān viddhi na tvahaṁ teṣhu te mayi

13

tribhir guṇa-mayair bhāvair ebhiḥ sarvam idaṁ jagat
mohitaṁ nābhijānāti māmebhyaḥ param avyayam

14

daivī hyeṣhā guṇa-mayī mama māyā duratyayā
mām eva ye prapadyante māyām etāṁ taranti te

15

na māṁ duṣhkṛitino mūḍhāḥ prapadyante narādhamāḥ
māyayāpahṛita-jñānā āsuraṁ bhāvam āśhritāḥ

16

chatur-vidhā bhajante māṁ janāḥ sukṛitino 'rjuna
ārto jijñāsur arthārthī jñānī cha bharatarṣhabha

17

teṣhāṁ jñānī nitya-yukta eka-bhaktir viśhiṣhyate
priyo hi jñānino 'tyartham ahaṁ sa cha mama priyaḥ

18

udārāḥ sarva evaite jñānī tvātmaiva me matam
āsthitaḥ sa hi yuktātmā mām evānuttamāṁ gatim

19

bahūnāṁ janmanām ante jñānavān māṁ prapadyate
vāsudevaḥ sarvam iti sa mahātmā su-durlabhaḥ

20

kāmais tais tair hṛita-jñānāḥ prapadyante 'nya-devatāḥ
taṁ taṁ niyamam āsthāya prakṛityā niyatāḥ svayā

21

yo yo yāṁ yāṁ tanuṁ bhaktaḥ śhraddhayārchitum ichchhati
tasya tasyāchalāṁ śhraddhāṁ tām eva vidadhāmyaham

22

sa tayā śhraddhayā yuktas tasyārādhanam īhate
labhate cha tataḥ kāmān mayaiva vihitān hi tān

23

antavat tu phalaṁ teṣhāṁ tad bhavatyalpa-medhasām
devān deva-yajo yānti mad-bhaktā yānti mām api

24

avyaktaṁ vyaktim āpannaṁ manyante mām abuddhayaḥ
paraṁ bhāvam ajānanto mamāvyayam anuttamam

25

nāhaṁ prakāśhaḥ sarvasya yoga-māyā-samāvṛitaḥ
mūḍho 'yaṁ nābhijānāti loko mām ajam avyayam

26

vedāhaṁ samatītāni vartamānāni chārjuna
bhaviṣhyāṇi cha bhūtāni māṁ tu veda na kaśhchana

27

ichchhā-dveṣha-samutthena dvandva-mohena bhārata
sarva-bhūtāni sammohaṁ sarge yānti parantapa

28

yeṣhāṁ tvanta-gataṁ pāpaṁ janānāṁ puṇya-karmaṇām
te dvandva-moha-nirmuktā bhajante māṁ dṛiḍha-vratāḥ

29

jarā-maraṇa-mokṣhāya mām āśhritya yatanti ye
te brahma tadviduḥ kṛitsnam adhyātmaṁ karma chākhilam

30

sādhibhūtādhidaivaṁ māṁ sādhiyajñaṁ cha ye viduḥ
prayāṇa-kāle 'pi cha māṁ te vidur yukta-chetasaḥ

Contact

9839093003

myrichindia@gmail.com

facebook.com/drjagadeeshpillaiofficial

youtube.com/drjagadeeshpillai

9 798888 494714

Printed by Libri Plureos GmbH in Hamburg, Germany